Guide Dogs

101 FACTS ABOUT GUIDE DOGS

Published by First Stone Publishing,
an imprint of Corpus Publishing Limited,
Unit 4/5 The Marina, Harbour Road, Lydney,
Gloucestershire, GL15 5ET,
United Kingdom.

Design: Sarah Williams

Cover design: Sara Howell

First Published 2003

ISBN 1 904439 098

Printed in Hong Kong through Printworks Int. Ltd

0 9 8 7 6 5 4 3 2 1

It is wonderful to see a guide dog striding out confidently, leading his blind owner through crowds of people and busy streets. But have you ever stopped to think about how it all works?

Who trains the guide dog? How does the dog know where to go? Can a dog really be trusted to lead his blind owner in heavy traffic?

There are around 5,000 guide dogs working in the UK, and there is always a demand for more. Despite all the advances in technology, a dog still remains the most effective guide for a blind person.

A guide dog gives his owner independence, love and loyalty – and that's a deal that will never be equalled.

1 Dogs have been helping to guide blind people for nearly 2,000 years. There is a wall painting in Pompeii, Italy, dating back to 79AD, which shows a dog leading his blind owner.

2 But it was not until the First World War (1914-1918) that there was an organised scheme dedicated to training dogs for blind people. The scheme started in Germany, when the Red Cross Ambulance Association used dogs to find the wounded in battlefields.

3 The dogs worked so well in the battlefields that it was quickly realised that they could be trained for other uses. Many soldiers were blinded in the First World War, and so the Red Cross dogs were trained to be their guides.

4 By 1919, more than 500 blind war veterans had guide dogs. Most of them were German Shepherds (pictured right).

5 A special training school was set up in Potsdam, Germany, and, by the 1930s, there were 4,000 German Shepherds working as guide dogs.

6 The school was visited by Dorothy Eustis, an American who specialised in breeding and training German Shepherds for the police, the army, and the customs service.

7 Dorothy was so impressed by what she saw, that, when she returned to her home in Switzerland, she trained two of her own German Shepherds as guide dogs.

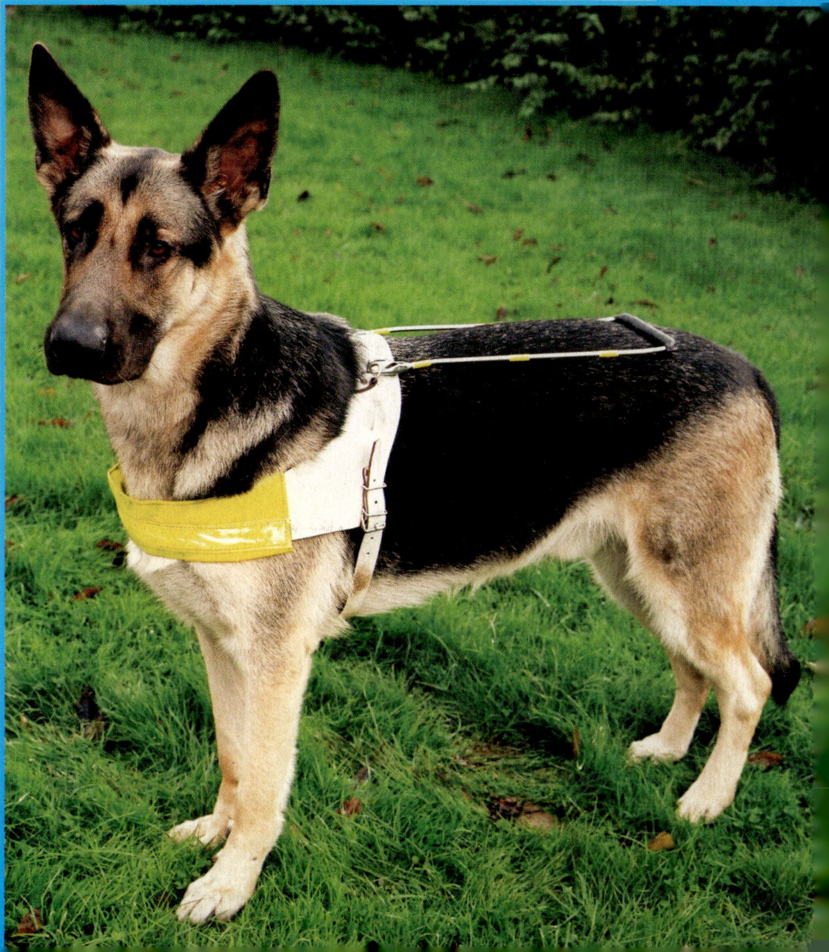

8 One of the dogs was called Buddy, and he went to work for an American called Morris Frank. Buddy made such a difference to Morris, he was determined that more blind people should have guide dogs.

9 Morris went back to the USA with Buddy, where he was soon joined by Dorothy Eustis. Together, they set to work and developed The Seeing Eye organisation, which remains one of the leading guide dog establishments in the US to this day.

10 In 1931, one of the instructors from The Seeing Eye, William Debetaz, was sent to England to train four British guide dogs and their owners.

11 It was their early success that led to the founding of The Guide Dogs for the Blind Association in the UK. But it was a long haul from these small beginnings to today's success story, with some 750 guide dogs being trained each year.

12 The biggest problem was finding enough dogs with the correct temperament and intelligence to be trained as guide dogs.

13 German Shepherds were favoured, but other breeds, such as Airedales (pictured left), Dalmatians, and Border Collies, were also tried.

14 A Boxer (pictured below), a Rough Collie, and an Alaskan Malamute were some of the more surprising breeds that qualified as guide dogs.

15 Today, the world is a much busier place, and today's guide dogs have a tougher job than those first dogs that went into training.

16 There are a number of qualities that every guide dog must have in order to do his job properly.

17 A guide dog must be willing to work, and be able to use his own initiative. He must also listen to his owner and respond to commands.

18 Often, guide dogs work in heavy traffic (pictured below right), so a calm dog, unworried by noise, is essential.

19 A shy or frightened dog is no good for guide dog work, and neither is a dog that shows aggression. Guide dogs must be confident and sociable.

20 A guide dog works in all sorts of different situations, so he must be prepared to get on with people of all ages, and live peaceably with other animals (pictured right).

21 It could be disastrous if a guide dog tried to run after a cat or another dog, so dogs that are chosen for training must show little or no interest in chasing.

22 A guide dog often needs to work in a place that is full of interesting sights and smells, and so he must be able to resist temptation and concentrate on his job.

23 All guide dogs must be fit and healthy, with a coat that is easy to care for. They must also be the right size to guide their owners. The smallest dogs accepted for training are 19 inches (47.5 cm) tall at the shoulder.

24 It is not easy to find a breed that matches all these requirements, but the Labrador Retriever (pictured left) probably comes very close.

25 Each breed has something special to bring to guide dog work. More than half of the guide dogs that are trained are Labradors, or first crosses with the Golden Retriever; around 12 per cent are Golden Retrievers, and German Shepherds make up eight per cent.

26 The Labrador Retriever is easy-going, friendly and willing, and suits a wide range of blind owners.

27 The Golden Retriever (pictured bottom right with a Labrador) has a kind, gentle character. He is slightly more sensitive than the Labrador.

28 The German Shepherd (pictured left) is a thinking dog, who thrives on a big workload. Guide dog owners who have had a German Shepherd often ask for another Shepherd when their dog retires.

29 If two breeds are crossed together, you can often get the best qualities from each breed. The Labrador/Golden Retriever cross has the highest success rate of the breeds that go into training.

30 Labradors have also been crossed with Curly Coated Retrievers (pictured below), and this has produced a dog that works well for many blind owners.

31 A small number of Border Collies (pictured above right) have also been trained as guide dogs.

32 The noble-looking Leonberger (pictured right) is a kindly, even-tempered dog, and bitches (who do not grow too big) are occasionally used.

33 A huge amount of time, money, and hard work goes into training guide dogs, and so it is vitally important to find not only the breeds that are suitable, but also the type of dog that will be happy to work.

34 The breakthrough for The Guide Dogs for the Blind Association came when they started breeding their own dogs. This began on a very small scale in the 1960s, and now more than 90 per cent of guide dogs are home-bred.

35 The very best dogs are chosen to be brood bitches and stud dogs, and they are matched so that the puppies they produce are most likely to have the qualities that are needed for guide dog work.

36 Both male and female puppies can become guide dogs. They are neutered before they complete their training.

37 The guide dog breeding programme now has 250 brood bitches, and 50 stud dogs. They live in family homes, and are called in when they are needed for mating. Nearly all brood bitches have their puppies at home (pictured top right).

38 Generally, each brood bitch will have four litters, and often, a pup from her third or fourth litter will be selected to replace her as a brood when she retires.

39 Each year, around 1,000 guide dog puppies are born. It would be hard to keep track of so many puppies, so each litter is identified by a letter of the alphabet.

40 This means that all pups in a litter will have names beginning with the chosen letter. There are lots of names to choose from, but a bit of imagination

is needed with the I and Y litters!

41 When the puppies are six weeks old, it is time to leave their mother and their brothers and sisters, and start their new lives as trainee guide dogs.

42 Each puppy is placed with a puppy walker, a volunteer who is specially selected to look after the pup until he is ready for advanced training.

43 The pup will live with the puppy walker's family until he is just over a year old. During this time, he will receive regular visits from a puppy walking supervisor, to check on his progress.

44 The puppy walker's job is to teach the pup basic obedience, starting with house-training, and progressing to simple training exercises.

45 The pup will learn good manners, such as sleeping in his own bed, not stealing or begging for food, not jumping up, and not barking too much. He must learn to live with other pets in the family (pictured below right), and to accept being groomed and handled.

46 The main work of the puppy walker is outside the home. To begin with, the pup must learn to walk calmly on a lead without pulling.

47 Pet dogs are trained to walk to heel, but guide dogs must work in a position just in front of the handler. A guide dog puppy will learn this position from the start of his lead-training.

48 A guide dog puppy needs to get used to the sound of traffic, and to moving among crowds.

49 The puppy must be happy to travel in a car and on a train and bus. He should also get used to the hurly burly of a bus or railway station (pictured right).

50 When he is on the lead, a guide dog puppy must not sniff or scavenge for food. This can be very difficult, especially for Labradors, who always seem to be hungry!

51 It is also important that the puppy ignores other dogs when he is out working.

52 But it is not all hard work for the guide dog trainees. They get plenty of play and exercise, and they have all the fun of being brought up in a loving family (pictured above).

53 When the pup is fully grown, usually at around 14 months of age (pictured below), he is ready for advanced training.

54 The puppy walker will hear how the pup is getting on throughout his training. If he becomes a fully-fledged guide dog, the puppy walker is given a special photo of the dog in harness with his new owner.

55 Very often, the guide dog

owner keeps in touch with the puppy walker, which has resulted in many long-lasting friendships.

56 Puppy walking is a mixture of fun, hard work, and a few tears, but most people find it very rewarding and go on to meet the challenge many times.

57 The more experienced puppy walkers are given the breeds that are slightly harder to train, such as German Shepherds or Curly Coated Retrievers.

58 The specialised work of training a guide dog takes around nine months. The trainers work with just a few dogs (pictured above), so that they can give them all the attention they need.

59 The first job is to get to know each dog, finding out his strengths and his weaknesses.

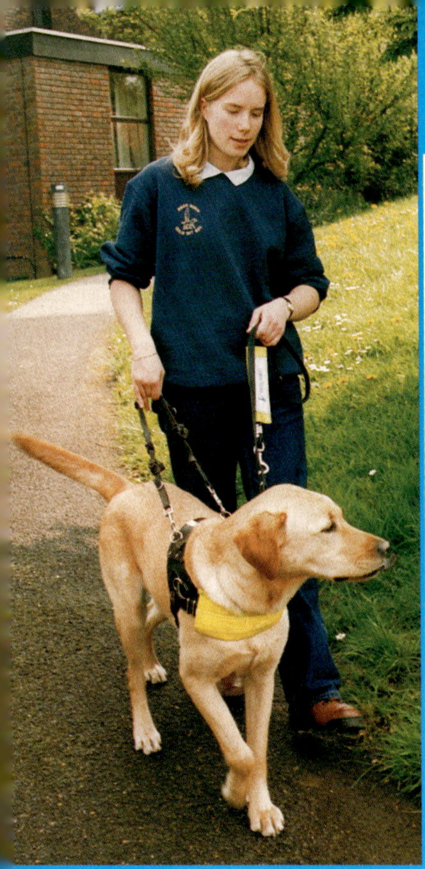

60 Early training is carried out on a long lead, so that the dog maintains guiding position. He will learn that the command "Hup-up" means speed up a little, while "Steady" means slow down.

61 After a few weeks, the trainee will be fitted with the body part of his harness, which has no handle (pictured above).

62 At this stage, the dog will also work on basic obedience commands, such as "Sit", "Down", "Stay", "Wait", and "Leave", so that he is well-behaved and responds to his handler.

63 The guide dog must also learn to change direction when he is asked. The handler (pictured right) gives a hand signal, and places her feet in the correct position so that the dog understands what is required.

64 The dog will learn that “Forward” means go forward from the Sit or Stand position; “Straight On” means keep on a straight line.

65 "Over” is used to encourage the dog to the left a little, and “In” means move to the right. The commands “Right”, “Left”, and “Back” are given from the standstill, and they indicate a complete change of direction.

66 It takes a lot of hard work and patience for a dog to learn these commands, and this is where the skill of the instructor is vital. The dog needs to enjoy working in order to give his best.

67 The trainee is now ready to be introduced to a harness (pictured below), and many instructors have found that the dog has a different attitude when he is wearing it. He knows the harness means he is working, and, when it is taken off, he can relax.

68 Learning to negotiate obstacles is the next stage of training (pictured above). Sometimes, a pavement is blocked because of road works or other construction work.

69 The guide dog must learn to stop at the obstacle, and then find a route past it. The path he takes must be wide enough and high enough for his handler to walk through safely.

70 The last and most difficult phase of training involves negotiating traffic. The trainee guide dog has learned to work confidently in heavy traffic, but now he has to go one step further.

71 It is the handler (pictured right) who makes the decision to cross a road. But the dog must learn to ignore the command to go "Forward" if a moving vehicle is too close. Even if the "Forward" command is repeated, the dog must ignore it until the road is clear.

72 This is the most advanced part of the training. A second instructor drives a car, so the dog can practise again and again.

73 In the last few weeks of training, the instructor will wear a blindfold on training walks, and another instructor will watch their progress.

74 The blindfolded handler (pictured above) cannot give any help to the dog, such as slowing up when approaching an obstacle, so the dog must cope on his own.

75 As training progresses, the instructor will find that some dogs are not quite right for guide dog work.

76 A dog may lack confidence when he is working in traffic, or he may find it difficult to concentrate for long periods.

77 Increasingly, dogs that are not suitable as guide dogs have a career change. Many go to work as assistance dogs for disabled

people (pictured left), and some go to the police and work as sniffer dogs.

78 The dogs that complete their training are now ready to be matched with their new owners. This is a very important decision, as the success of the partnership will depend on how well the dog and the blind person suit each other.

79 The needs of each blind person are different. This may depend on age, health, or the type of work they do. Some guide dog owners have a very active lifestyle (pictured above), while others take life at a slower pace.

80 It takes a great deal of skill to find the right match, but training a number of different breeds, which have slightly different qualities to offer, helps this process.

large groups of children if his owner is a teacher.

82 One of Britain's most famous – and busiest – guide dog owners is David Blunkett MP (pictured left), who is currently Home Secretary. He has a hectic schedule, packed with engagements, but his dog, Sadie, is more than equal to the task.

81 Sometimes, a dog will need extra, specialised training. For example, he may need to get used to travelling on the London Underground if his owner commutes to work, or he may need to get used to

83 Sadie, a Labrador/Curly Coated Retriever cross, has taken over from Lucy, who has now gone into well-deserved retirement.

84 When a good 'match' has been worked out, it is time for the guide dog to meet his new owner. This can be a very emotional moment, as it is the start of a new partnership, which will change both their lives dramatically.

85 It takes around four weeks to train a blind owner with his new dog (pictured right). This is often done at the owner's home, where the whole family can be on hand to help and support the new partnership.

86 It also means that the dog and handler can learn the routes to and from work, to the shops, and to other places that are visited regularly.

87 Right from the start, the guide dog is cared for by his new owner. This helps to build up the relationship between them.

88 It is also important that the new owner understands what his dog needs in terms of feeding, grooming and exercise.

89 New guide dog owners (pictured above) have a lot to learn.

In order to work with a guide dog, the blind handler must learn the voice commands, the hand signals, and the foot positions, so that the dog will understand what he is supposed to do.

90 The dog could easily get confused during this learning stage, and so the instructor plays the part of the dog while the blind person learns the basics.

91 Now comes the hardest part of the training. The blind owner starts to work with his new dog, and this means the dog

has to transfer his loyalty from the instructor to his new handler.

92 The instructor is skilled at making this changeover as easy as possible, so that the dog learns to look to his new owner for praise, rather than to the instuctor.

93 As the training progresses, the blind person becomes more skilled at handling the dog, and they start to work together as a team (pictured right). It is at this point that they begin to work in busier, more challenging situations.

94 After four weeks of hard work, the partnership is ready to start their working life together (pictured below). The instructor will continue to make regular visits to check that both the guide dog and owner are working well together.

95 Usually, a guide dog will work for the next seven years. During this time, he will live a busy and rewarding life. His main job will be working as a guide, but he will also have plenty of free time for play and exercise (pictured above).

96 When a guide dog is ready to retire, his owner will be re-trained with a new guide dog. Often, the retired guide dog will stay in the family as a much-loved pet.

97 Most guide dog owners say that the older dog is quite happy to 'hang up his harness', and let the younger dog take over.

98 There is a long waiting list of people who want to adopt a retired guide dog, and so if the dog has to move on, he will be sure of a loving home where he will be cared for to the end of his life.

99 It costs £35,000 to breed, train and support each guide dog, so you can imagine how difficult it is to find enough money to pay for all the guide dogs that are so desperately needed.

100 Fortunately, many people are prepared to work hard for Guide Dogs. There are around 300 local branches, which specialise in fundraising, and there are lots of pubs, clubs, schools and stores that collect money for the charity.

101 It is vital that Guide Dogs get all the support they need, so that they can carry on their remarkable work, transforming the lives of thousands of blind people.

MORE ABOUT GUIDE DOGS

The Pups Club

If you enjoyed this book, why not join the Guide Dogs Pups Club? You can follow the adventures of five cartoon Guide Dog puppies – Pippa, Prince, Peds, Paddy and Penny – and find out the pet secrets of your favourite pop stars. There are also great competitions to enter. Find out more on the Pups website at **www.pupsclub.org.uk**

Shades for a Day

How cool are you? Here's a great chance for you to raise money to help Guide Dogs and to learn about keeping your eyes safe in the sun. It's simple: you pay £1 to wear your sunglasses to school – 50p comes to Guide Dogs and 50p to your school fund. Why not ask your teacher if you can take part? Log on to **www.shadesforaday.org.uk** and find out about Guide Dogs' healthy eyes campaign.

More to read

Goldie becomes a guide dog and ***Pippa takes the lead***: two great booklets about puppies who grow up to be guide dogs.

And your teacher will love the ***Primary Pups Education Pack*** – make lessons fun, learning about Guide Dogs and how you can help people who are blind or who cannot see well.

Call 0870 600 2323* for more details or log on to **www.guidedogs.org.uk***

(*Calls are charged at national rate)
Remember to ask the bill payer's permission before calling or clicking